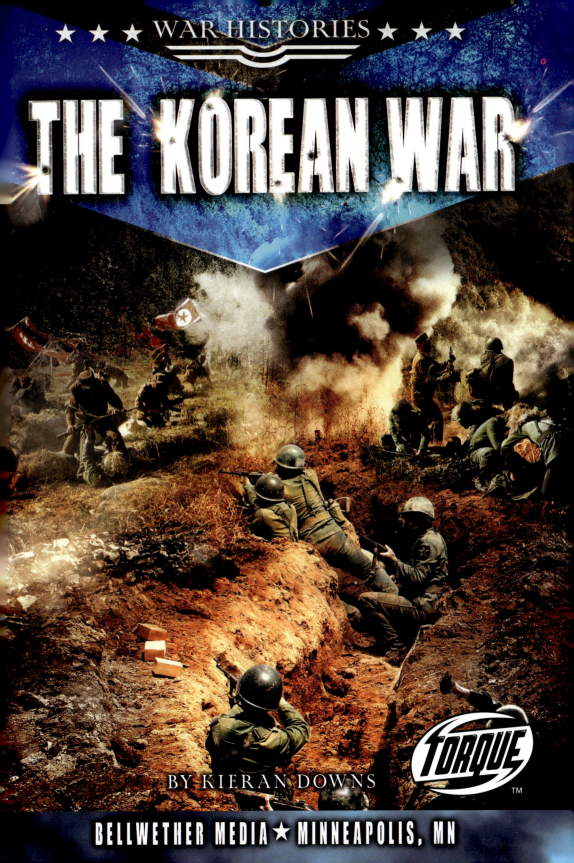

Torque brims with excitement perfect for thrill-seekers of all kinds. Discover daring survival skills, explore uncharted worlds, and marvel at mighty engines and extreme sports. In *Torque* books, anything can happen. Are you ready?

This edition first published in 2025 by Bellwether Media, Inc.

No part of this publication may be reproduced in whole or in part without written permission of the publisher. For information regarding permission, write to Bellwether Media, Inc., Attention: Permissions Department, 6012 Blue Circle Drive, Minnetonka, MN 55343.

Library of Congress Cataloging-in-Publication Data

Names: Downs, Kieran, author.
Title: The Korean War / by Kieran Downs.
Description: Minneapolis, MN : Bellwether Media, 2025. | Series: Torque: War Histories | Includes bibliographical references and index. | Audience: Ages 7-12 | Audience: Grades 4-6 | Summary: "Engaging images accompany information about the Korean War. The combination of high-interest subject matter and light text is intended for students in grades 3 through 7"– Provided by publisher.
Identifiers: LCCN 2024035372 (print) | LCCN 2024035373 (ebook) | ISBN 9798893042733 (library binding) | ISBN 9798893044171 (paperback) | ISBN 9798893043709 (ebook)
Subjects: LCSH: Korean War, 1950-1953–Juvenile literature.
Classification: LCC DS918 .D69 2025 (print) | LCC DS918 (ebook) | DDC 951.904/24–dc23/eng/20240801
LC record available at https://lccn.loc.gov/2024035372
LC ebook record available at https://lccn.loc.gov/2024035373

Text copyright © 2025 by Bellwether Media, Inc. TORQUE and associated logos are trademarks and/or registered trademarks of Bellwether Media, Inc.

Editor: Rebecca Sabelko   Designer: Josh Brink

Printed in the United States of America, North Mankato, MN.

TABLE OF CONTENTS

WHAT WAS THE KOREAN WAR?	4
ONE LAND, TWO NATIONS	6
THE WAR BEGINS	10
THE WAR SLOWS	14
AN UNEASY PEACE	18
GLOSSARY	22
TO LEARN MORE	23
INDEX	24

WHAT WAS THE KOREAN WAR?

The Korean War was from 1950 to 1953. It was fought on the Korean **peninsula** between North Korea and South Korea. It was part of the **Cold War**.

★ KOREAN WAR MAP ★

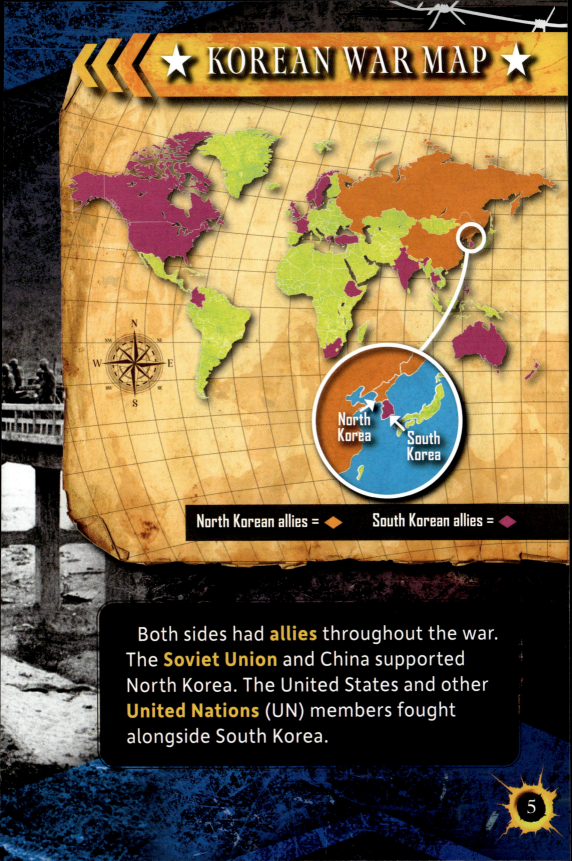

North Korean allies = ◆   South Korean allies = ◆

Both sides had **allies** throughout the war. The **Soviet Union** and China supported North Korea. The United States and other **United Nations** (UN) members fought alongside South Korea.

ONE LAND, TWO NATIONS

The Japanese **Empire** took over Korea in 1910. The Empire fell in 1945 after Japan lost in **World War II**. The U.S. and the Soviet Union took over the peninsula.

JAPAN'S DEFEAT IN WORLD WAR II

NORTH KOREAN LEADER

NAME
Kim Il Sung

NATIONALITY
North Korean

RANK
North Korean Prime Minister (1948 to 1972)

IMPORTANT ACTIONS
- 1948: Became the leader of North Korea
- 1950: Invaded South Korea
- 1953: Signed the Armistice Agreement

An imaginary line called the 38th parallel divided North Korea and South Korea. The Soviet Union occupied the north. The U.S. claimed the south.

By 1948, the Soviet Union supported Kim Il Sung as the leader of North Korea. He formed a **communist** government. The UN pushed for an independent South Korea. The U.S. backed Syngman Rhee as its leader. He stood against communism.

SYNGMAN RHEE WITH A U.S. MILITARY LEADER

SOUTH KOREAN LEADER

NAME
Syngman Rhee

NATIONALITY
South Korean

RANK
South Korean President (1948 to 1960)

IMPORTANT ACTIONS
- 1948: Became the leader of South Korea
- 1951: Retook Seoul
- 1953: Signed the Armistice Agreement

Both countries wanted more land. Many smaller fights broke out between them.

THE WAR BEGINS

On June 25, 1950, North Korea **invaded** South Korea. They quickly took much of the peninsula. On June 28, the South Korean capital of Seoul fell.

U.S. TROOPS IN THE BATTLE OF THE PUSAN PERIMETER

NOT A WAR

The U.S. never declared war on North Korea.

BATTLE OF THE PUSAN PERIMETER

North Korea

Sea of Japan

South Korea

North Korean forces =
Pusan Perimeter =
38th parallel =

The U.S. and other UN forces arrived to help South Korea. Together, they formed the Pusan Perimeter. They held this area along the Sea of Japan. It allowed the UN to receive troops and supplies.

On September 15, UN forces began the Inchon Landing. This helped South Korea gain ground. They retook Seoul by September 26. UN forces pushed north. But China began to worry about its border.

INCHON LANDING

HIGGINS BOAT

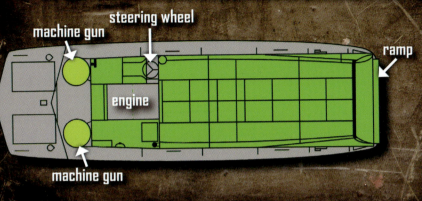

UN forces used Higgins boats during the Inchon Landing. These boats helped them reach land while under fire.

China attacked through the beginning of 1951. China and North Korea retook areas. They took over the capital again. But UN forces pushed back.

THE WAR SLOWS

In May 1951, UN forces took the capital again. Fighting returned to the 38th parallel. It became clear fighting would not bring an end to the war.

SECRET FIGHTERS

The Soviet Union never officially joined the war. But they sent fighter pilots to fight for North Korea.

1951 PEACE TALKS

In July, peace talks began. But no agreement was reached. Fighting continued around the 38th parallel for the next two years. But neither side gained ground.

In 1953, peace talks began again. Both sides signed the **Armistice Agreement** on July 27. This brought an end to the fighting. It also allowed prisoners to return home.

The agreement created a **demilitarized zone** on the 38th parallel. **Civilians** were not allowed to cross it from either side. This broke up many families.

KOREAN WAR TIMELINE

1945
Korea is given to the Soviet Union and United States

June 25, 1950
North Korea invades South Korea

September 15, 1950
The Inchon Landing pushes back North Korean troops

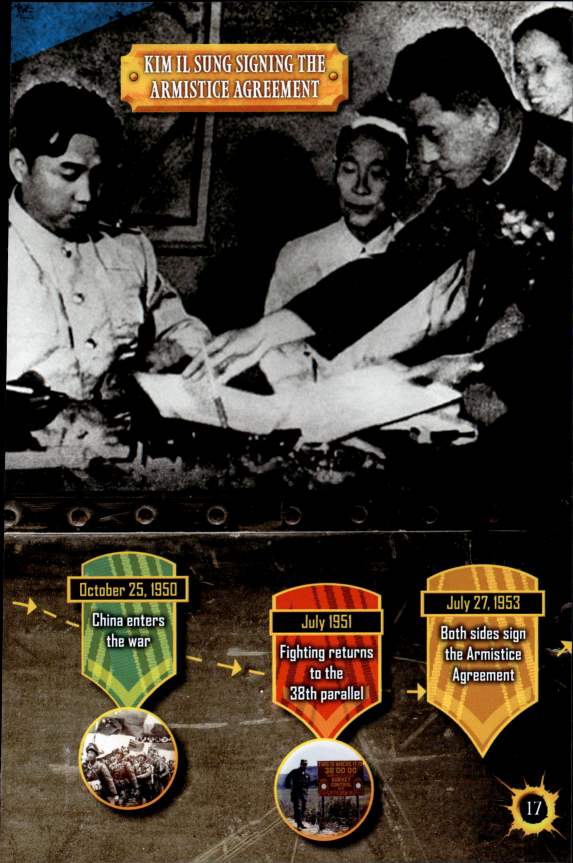

AN UNEASY PEACE

More than 1.5 million troops died or went missing during the war. Even more civilians died or were never seen again.

MISSING IN ACTION

Thousands of troops went missing in the war. Around 7,500 U.S. troops are still missing.

THE WAR AT HOME

The U.S. used a draft to get troops for the war. Drafts order people of a country to join that country's military. Around 1.5 million soldiers were drafted. The most came in 1951. Over 550,000 men were drafted in that year.

In the U.S., the Korean War is known as the "Forgotten War." People were often uncaring towards returning troops. Many people did not even know where they had been.

North Korea is still a communist country. Many people struggle to live well. South Korea has a growing **economy**. People work to build successful farms and businesses.

An official end to the Korean War has never been declared. North and South Korea have talked about becoming one nation. But the two countries remain separate.

SEOUL, SOUTH KOREA

★ BY THE NUMBERS ★

10,000 people =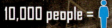

ESTIMATED DEATHS AND MISSING PERSONS

- South Korean troops: 217,000
- South Korean civilians: 1,000,000
- North Korean troops: 406,000
- North Korean civilians: 600,000
- UN personnel: more than 39,000
- Chinese troops: 600,000

MAIN COUNTRIES INVOLVED

- South Korea and 20 UN member nations
- North Korea, China, Soviet Union

TOTAL U.S. MILITARY PERSONNEL SENT TO KOREA

- 1,789,000

COST OF THE KOREAN WAR TO THE U.S.

- around $353 billion (in 2024 dollars)

GLOSSARY

allies—countries that support and help other countries in a war

Armistice Agreement—an agreement between North Korea and South Korea to stop fighting

civilians—people who do not belong to a nation's armed forces

Cold War—a conflict between the U.S. and Soviet Union in the second half of the 1900s that did not break out into fighting

communist—related to communism; communism is a social system in which property and goods are controlled by the government.

demilitarized zone—an area in which weapons and military forces have been removed

economy—the way a country makes, sells, and uses goods and services

empire—a group of people led by one ruler

invaded—entered a land and controlled it

peninsula—a section of land that extends out from a larger piece of land and is completely surrounded by water

Soviet Union—a country in eastern Europe and northern Asia from 1922 to 1991

United Nations—a political group formed in 1945 that works around the world to maintain peace

World War II—the war fought from 1939 to 1945 that involved many countries

TO LEARN MORE

AT THE LIBRARY

McKinney, Donna. *The United States Army*. Minneapolis, Minn.: Bellwether Media, 2025.

Moening, Kate. *The Cold War*. Minneapolis, Minn.: Bellwether Media, 2024.

Monroe, Alex. *World War II*. Minneapolis, Minn.: Bellwether Media, 2024.

ON THE WEB

FACTSURFER

Factsurfer.com gives you a safe, fun way to find more information.

1. Go to www.factsurfer.com

2. Enter "Korean War" into the search box and click 🔍.

3. Select your book cover to see a list of related content.

INDEX

38th parallel, 7, 14, 15, 16
allies, 5
Armistice Agreement, 16, 17
by the numbers, 21
China, 5, 12, 13
civilians, 16, 18
Cold War, 4
communist government, 8, 20
demilitarized zone, 16
economy, 20
Higgins boat, 13
Il Sung, Kim, 7, 8, 17
Inchon Landing, 12
Japanese Empire, 6
leaders, 7, 9
map, 5, 11
name, 19
North Korea, 4, 5, 7, 8, 9, 10, 13, 14, 20
peace talks, 15, 16
peninsula, 4, 6, 10
Pusan Perimeter, 10, 11
Rhee, Syngman, 8, 9
Sea of Japan, 11
Seoul, 10, 12, 13, 14, 20
South Korea, 4, 5, 7, 8, 9, 10, 11, 12, 20
Soviet Union, 5, 6, 7, 8, 14
timeline, 16–17
troops, 10, 11, 18, 19
United Nations, 5, 8, 11, 12, 13, 14
United States, 5, 6, 7, 8, 10, 11, 18, 19
war at home, 19
World War II, 6

The images in this book are reproduced through the courtesy of: AFP/ Getty Images, front cover (battle scene), pp. 4-5; Defense Visual Information Distribution Service/ NARA & DVIDS, front cover (medic top right, North Korean soldiers); US Army Photo/ Alamy, pp. 2-3, 22-24; MPI/ Stringer/ Getty Images, pp. 6-7; RBM Vintage Images/ Alamy, p. 7; Library of Congress/ Getty Images, pp. 8-9; Harris & Ewing/ Wiki Commons, p. 9; AB Historic/ Alamy, pp. 10-11; Bettmann/ Getty Images, pp. 12-13, 14-15, 18-19, 19; American Soldier/ Newscom, p. 13; Fred the Oyster/ Wiki Commons, p. 13 (Higgins boat); Air Force Declassification Office, p. 15; National Archives/ U.S. Department of Defense, pp. 16-17; USMC Archives/ Wiki Commons, p. 16 (September 15, 1950); Universal History Archive/ Getty Images, p. 17 (November 25, 1950); Sydney M. Schaer, M.D./ Getty Images, p. 17 (July 1951); Roussel Bernard/ Alamy, pp. 20-21.